D1458363

Other titles in the series:
The Crazy World of Cats (Bill Stott)
The Crazy World of Cricket (Bill Stott)
The Crazy World of Gardening (Bill Stott)
The Crazy World of Golf (Mike Scott)
The Crazy World of the Greens (Barry Knowles)
The Crazy World of the Handyman (Roland Fiddy)
The Crazy World of Housework (Bill Stott)
The Crazy World of Marriage (Bill Stott)
The Crazy World of Rugby (Bill Stott)
The Crazy World of Sailing (Peter Rigby)
The Crazy World of Sex (David Pye)

This paperback edition published simultaneously in 1992 by Exley
Publications Ltd. in Great Britain, and Exley Giftbooks in the USA.
First hardback edition published in Great Britain in 1990 by Exley
Publications Ltd.

Copyright © Bill Stott, 1990

ISBN 1-85015-357-4

Printed in Spain by Grafo S.A., Bilbao.

Exley Publications Ltd, 16 Chalk Hill, Watford, Herts WD1 4BN,
United Kingdom.
Exley Giftbooks, 359 East Main Street, Suite 3D, Mount Kisco,
NY 10549, USA.

the CRAZY world of HOSPITALS

Cartoons by
Bill Stott

EXLEY

MT. KISCO, NEW YORK • WATFORD, UK

"*You know, for a moment there, I got the distinct impression that you didn't want me to take these off.*"

"Poor Mr. Hardacre's got to have another enema ..."

"A little tense today, Mr. Fairbrother?"

"*I've had a terrible time. I was so ill, I didn't even want to talk about it!*"

"… and the lady at Number 47 with the big chests has made Daddy three cakes and one of those lasagnes you hate …"

"*I've told you before – no more wheelies!*"

"You'll have to speak up – 'piles' did you say?"

"*Nothing wrong with your reflexes ...*"

"Staff shortage."

"Interesting case in Number One for you Doc ..."

"Now, you'll just feel a slight ..."

"One of the hidden pitfalls of private medicine, I'm afraid –
I've found out what's wrong with you, but I won't tell you
unless you pay double."

HOSPITAL 4 MILES   VISITORS' PARKING

"They only ever cry at visiting time ..."

"Valve's stuck …"

"Fifty years married and never a night of fun – until now!"

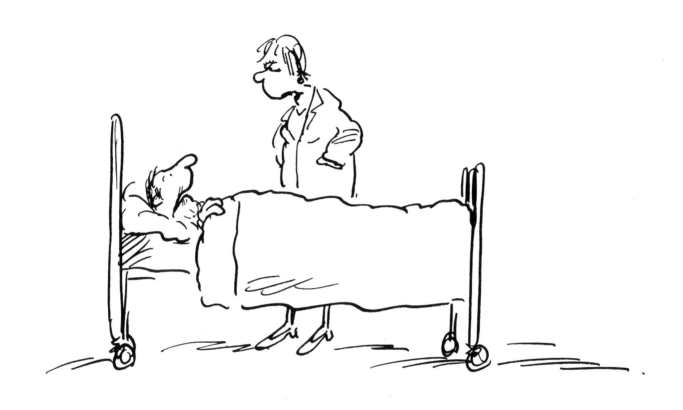

"Well, we've had the results of the tests Mr. Fittock and I have to tell you that you have nothing famous."

"*Well, it was a sort of white-hot agony searing my whole being to the point of unconsciousness. Now it's receding like a purple curtain of pain, a sweeping tide of physical discomfort reforming, preparing for the next awful onslaught.*"

"Here's a list of things to talk about for tomorrow. Learn it."

"Hi there, I'm Chief Surgeon Tom Berkowicz. I'll be taking care of your little op. Today, on scalpels is Jennifer Webb. Looking after swabs is Nurse Jimmy Peters. Vital signs are ..."

"And whose idea was it to bring Aunt Eileen?"

"Have you got that one by our catering manager – 'Lives of the Great Poisoners'?"

"If you don't let me give you this suppository, I'll tell nurse what you said about her walk."

"I don't trust these surgeons – so I make them keep everything they take out."

"Doctor – about the youth brought in after being cut free from the park railings ..."

"For heaven's sake, Mr. Willoughby, you're only having your verruca trimmed!"

"Age? You mean now or when we first sat down?"

AND THEN ON MONDAY MRS WHATSERNAME RANG AND ASKED AFTER YOU JUST BEFORE DOREEN CALLED AND GUESS WHAT? THEIR GARY HAS FINALLY......
ZZZZZZZZZZZZZZZZ

"*That Mr. Stephenson is out of bed again. If he's smoking in the toilet, I'll …*"

"My social life affecting my work? What makes you say that, Nurse?"

THIS CABINET IS TIME LOCKED

Nurse Stebbings. Mr. Finch is excused bed-baths."

"Those? Banister rails. He didn't want to come."

"There's been some sort of mistake. He came to clean the windows."

"I know just the operation for you, Mr. Spendlove. Unfortunately, I don't think anybody has pulled off a whole body transplant yet."

"If we gave you <u>nice</u> food, you'd want to stay here instead of going home to your loved ones."

"I've been waiting so long, my stomach pains have cleared up.
I've got a headache now."

"When I said 'use your imagination' about bringing my clothes in, I did not mean one pair of dungarees, two left boots and a ski hat."

"That Mrs. Goodbody around the corner's having <u>another</u> dedication on the hospital radio."

"Two visitors per bed ..."

"That Nurse O'Hooligan hates visitors who pretend not to have heard the bell."

"This bleeper's got a mind of its own."

"*I know you feel sorry for Mr. Finningsby, but putting sandwiches in his ear really doesn't help.*"

"I told you it was a hair piece!"

"Now then – you're not frightened of me are you, little man?"

"Put that down as 'no', Nurse."

"Yes – that's my surgeon – the one who cuts himself shaving ..."

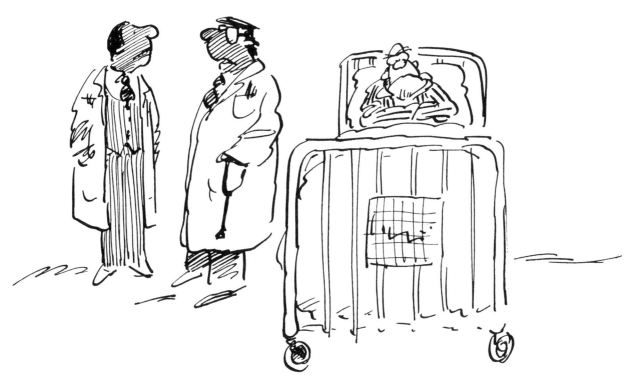

"He criticizes everything – the food, the staff – everything.
So I've put him on the critical list."

"What do you mean, you hate the smell of hospitals? You're the doctor!"

"George! It's a lady doctor ..."

"Didn't I tell you? That young blonde doctor
hates chauvinist remarks."

"Keep your eye on him: it's not every day you operate on your bank manager."

"*Brace yourself, son. When J.J. Farnsworth lances a boil – he lances a boil!*"

"He's got his father's nose."

"*Nurse Willoughby! During a bed-bath, only the patient is in the bed!*"

"Doctor, Doctor, Mr. Brunskill's showing off again."

"It's a type of suspended animation. We call it 'waiting'."

"*Yes, it is unfortunate – just don't go in any tough areas.*"

"*Come on, own up. <u>How</u> fast were you wheeling Mr. Goodacre?*"

"*I thought before we chatted you could run through the washing machine manual with me ...*"

"Name?"

"*Before I leave you to soak, Mr. Worthington, let me remind you that only at Sunnyview Private Clinic do you get boats in the bath.*"

"…. takes on a whole new meaning with Mr. Thornberry in charge …"

"*I can understand you feeling jealous of Mr. Pratt's hardware, but it wouldn't do your strangulated hernia any good at all.*"

"Make a note, Nurse Newman '9:40 a.m., pill cabinet leaking again'."

"My colleagues and I are baffled. We have no idea what's wrong with you – but would you mind nipping up to the children's ward – they love a good laugh."

"She's still not herself – she had me put the grapes in water
and then ate the daffodils ..."

"I've bitten the ends off more thermometers than you've had hot dinners tootsie."

"Well, it's not a <u>good</u> sign, that's for sure ..."

"Early morning alarm call Doctor?"

"Well you can have a look, but only if you close your eyes."

"We don't know what it is, but we do know it's contagious."

Books in the "Crazy World" series
($4.99 £2.99 paperback)

The Crazy World of Cats (Bill Stott)
The Crazy World of Cricket (Bill Stott)
The Crazy World of Gardening (Bill Stott)
The Crazy World of Golf (Mike Scott)
The Crazy World of the Greens (Barry Knowles)
The Crazy World of the Handyman (Roland Fiddy)
The Crazy World of Hospitals (Bill Stott)
The Crazy World of Housework (Bill Stott)
The Crazy World of Marriage (Bill Stott)
The Crazy World of Rugby (Bill Stott)
The Crazy World of Sailing (Peter Rigby)
The Crazy World of Sex (David Pye)

The Mini Joke Book series
($6.99 £3.99 hardback)

These attractive 64 page mini joke books are illustrated
in colour throughout by Bill Stott.

A Binge of Diet Jokes
A Bouquet of Wedding Jokes
A Feast of After Dinner Jokes
A Portfolio of Business Jokes
A Round of Golf Jokes
A Romp of Naughty Jokes
A Spread of Over-40s Jokes

The "Fanatics" series ($4.99 £2.99 paperback)

The **Fanatic's Guides** are perfect presents for everyone
with a hobby that has got out of hand. Eighty pages of
hilarious black and white cartoons by Roland Fiddy

The Fanatic's Guide to the Bed
The Fanatic's Guide to Cats
The Fanatic's Guide to Computers
The Fanatic's Guide to Dads
The Fanatic's Guide to Diets
The Fanatic's Guide to Dogs
The Fanatic's Guide to Husbands
The Fanatic's Guide to Money
The Fanatic's Guide to Sex
The Fanatic's Guide to Skiing

Great Britain: Order these super books from your local
bookseller or from Exley Publications Ltd, 16 Chalk
Hill, Watford, Herts WD1 4BN. (Please send £1.25 to
cover postage and packing on 1 book, £2.50 on 2 or
more books.)